MW01074982

A Spirituality for
Late Life

OLDER ADULT ISSUES SERIES

The Office of Older Adult Ministry of the Presbyterian Church (U.S.A.) and Geneva Press are grateful for the generous gifts of many individuals, congregations, and organizations that helped make possible the publication of this series.

A Spirituality for
Late Life

Juliana Cooper-Goldenberg

Published for the Office of Older Adult Ministry,
A Ministry of the General Assembly Council,
Presbyterian Church (U.S.A.)

Geneva Press
Louisville, Kentucky

© 1999 Office of Older Adult Ministry, Congregational Ministries Division, Presbyterian Church (U.S.A.)

All rights reserved. No part of this book may be reproduced or transmitted in any form or by any means, electronic or mechanical, including photocopying, recording, or by any information storage or retrieval system, without permission in writing from the publisher. For information, address Geneva Press, 100 Witherspoon Street, Louisville, Kentucky 40202-1396.

Portions of this book may be reproduced for not-for-profit use only.

Scripture quotations are from the New Revised Standard Version of the Bible, copyright © 1989 by the Division of Christian Education of the National Council of the Churches of Christ in the U.S.A., and are used by permission.

ISBN 0-664-50084-6

Prayer of Teresa of Avila

Trust in God.
Let nothing disturb you,
Let nothing frighten you;
All things pass.
God never changes.
Patience achieves all it strives for.
He [or she] who has God
Finds he [or she] lacks nothing.
God alone suffices.

Contents

Introduction

What are some of the issues relating to a third-age (age sixty and older) spirituality and the church's response to the growing numbers of elders in its ranks? The first issue that we must deal with is that aging is a normal part of life, not a pathology or problem to be responded to. For too long in this culture, we have viewed aging in pejorative ways, using language such as "over the hill" or "second childhood." We live in a society that persists in glorifying and worshiping youth, often forgetting to see the riches and gifts of late life. If we truly believe that we are created in the image of God, then that image must extend to all of the seasons of our lives.

Another important issue involves the need to shift our focus to ministry *with* the aging, not *to* the aging. That is an important piece of semantics. "With" implies a mutuality of ministry that is critical. During my twenty-two years of working with elders and their families, I have found that I have been ministered to *by* them far more than I have ministered *to* them. This ministry is a two-way street upon which we travel.

Remember that this ministry with the aging also implies that we are all on the journey of aging at different points; some of us are farther ahead, and some of us are just starting out. Seeing it as a ministry "with" also help us to get rid of some of the us-versus-them thinking that has been so damaging in our culture. Ministry "with" the aging implies that all parts of the life cycle are valuable and important. As Evelyn and James Whitehead write, "It takes a lifetime for God to show us who we are."

Another important point to keep in mind is the reality that the aging population is incredibly diverse and will likely tend to be even more diverse as the baby boomers hit late life. Along with that, we must also remember that late life spans four decades of our lives. These decades of life include everything from the most active and healthy to the most frail and vulnerable, and all conditions in between. This diversity is a challenge to all of us as we try to conceptualize the needs of elders, plan programs, and formulate policy at denominational and congregational levels.

We need to enlarge our vision of aging to include this incredible range and diversity if we are truly going to be able to understand and respond to this "age presence." We are often tempted to see late life as either a time of endless promise and opportunities for fulfillment, or as a time of pervasive loss, physical decline, and death. We must see late life in all of its facets if we are to reach a realistic view of aging. Aging is a paradox and we must understand this paradox if we are to fully understand late life.

The church is beginning to wake up and face the demographic revolution. We are beginning to look around and see the elders in our midst. We are beginning to ask how we should respond to their needs, and more important, how we can call forth their gifts. We are beginning to wonder if there is a distinct third-age spirituality and how the body of Christ should address it. We are beginning to ask how we can address notions of self-transcendence and vocation in late life. We are beginning to examine the needs of middle-aged caregivers for elderly relatives. We are beginning to dialogue about personal decisions related to aging and the end of our lives. We are beginning to struggle with creating meaningful roles for elders in our congregations.

The church, I believe, is the best place to start on our journey of creating a vision and a reality of aging that is positive, creative, and fulfilling. It is the place where we can work to make old age a vital time of animate existence, rather than a time of inevitable decline. But to do that, we must first understand the role of spirituality in late life. The church is not just a social service agency. As the body of Christ, we have a unique voice as it relates to aging, and the uniqueness of that voice is rooted in our understanding of the gospel and Christ's presence in our lives throughout our life span.

1 Issues of Spirituality in the Third Age

Let's take a look at the issues that surround spirituality in the third age of our lives. We'll start with a quote from C. G. Jung:

> We cannot live the afternoon of life according to the program of life's morning, for what was great in the morning will be little by the evening and what in the morning was true will of evening become a lie.[1]

There are needs and issues that are specific to our journey through late life that impact and influence our spirituality.

The Life Review

One of the most important issues is the "life review," which was first postulated by Robert Butler, M.D., some thirty years ago. It is a looking back at one's life, which becomes strikingly intense as our perceived proximity to death intensifies. We all reminisce; it is a lifelong activity, but it takes on greater intensity during late life. It is a universal process that can lead to growth for the individual, family, and community.

A very important part of this life review is the feelings that are associated with these memories and long-forgotten incidents. What we used to think of as pathologically living in the past or perhaps a second childhood, we now recognize as a vital task of the elder in coming to grips with his or her life. The process includes a progressive remembering of past experiences and revisiting unresolved conflicts. We are sometimes startled by the clarity of these memories; it is often literally as if the event had happened yesterday, rather than sixty years ago. This life review process is an important vehicle in defining the individual's identity and self-esteem, as well as a tool in helping one cope with current losses. It is a work of life harvesting, and the faith context provides it with great therapeutic power. As Kathleen Fischer writes, "We do not merely have these memories; we are these memories."[2]

The life review can be an important process in facilitating the growth of hope and courage. Arthur Becker writes about the life review: "A life review is like looking at the wake of our life and seeing the direction of God's guiding, caring nurture as He was at the helm of our life . . . the loving presence of God was there even in suffering."[3] If we can bring forward the healthy metaphors of the past into our current reality, they can become the source of expectation and hope as we move into the future, and into the vision of who God intends us to be. As Jane Thibault states, "Life review is a stabilization in the security of the past so that we can go beyond to embrace the future."[4]

The life review can become a confession of faith, a recounting of God's presence in our journeys. It can be the chance for the healing of memories, a time when individuals can reflect on God's presence even in the worst of memories, and a time when we can look at the areas that are asking for forgiveness. The spiritual context of life review can be an opportunity to let go and begin to be open to God's continuing action in our lives.

Frederick Buechner writes of the importance of seeking God in the midst of our stories and the stories of others. He writes, "If the God you believe in as an idea doesn't start showing up in what happens to you in your own life, you have as much cause for concern as if the God you don't believe in as an idea does start showing up. It is absolutely crucial, therefore, to keep in constant touch with what is going on in your own life's story and to pay close attention to what is going on in the stories of others' lives. If God is present anywhere, it is in those stories that God is present. If God is not present in those stories, then you might as well give up the whole business."[5] Story sharing connects us with our heritage, with those who journey with us now, and with the God of our stories. When we share the most personal stories, we allow others to connect at the deepest level of what it means to be a human being.

But there is also sadness associated with the life review. Myrna Lewis and Robert Butler write: "Life review, by its very nature, evokes a sense of regret and sadness at the brevity of life, the missed opportunities, the mistakes, the wrong doings to others, the chosen paths that turned out badly."[6] For many elders, the life review process will include having to face the secrets of their past, but these secrets call out to us to grapple with them in the context of supportive relationships.

This idea of the life review evokes the image of a tapestry.

May Sarton writes of this in the following passage: "In the middle of the night things well up from the past that are not always cause for rejoicing—the unsolved, the painful encounters, the mistakes, the reasons for shame or woe. But all, good or bad, painful or delightful, weave themselves into a rich tapestry, food to grow on."[7]

The Crisis of Integrity and Despair

The life review is integrally tied to a second important issue of late life spirituality: the crisis of ego integrity versus despair. This was postulated by Erik Erikson as the final crisis of a person's life and is described in this way: "It is the acceptance of one's own and only life cycle as something that had to be, and by necessity, permitted no substitutions . . . and an acceptance of the fact that one's life is one's own responsibility."[8] It is through the telling of the stories that the elder must come to an assessment of the worth of his or her life. Remember that this assessment is on a continuum. Ego integrity is the sense of completeness, coherence, and wholeness of one's life. It is not that there is an absence of regrets, but that there is a sense of integration. Despair focuses on lost opportunities, wrongdoings, and perhaps, most important, the lack of energy, time, and opportunity to change these.

Stress, Loss, and Limits

A third issue of late life involves dealing with the experience of limits. Most of what we consider stressful happens with increasing frequency to elders. These events include changes in health status, losing a spouse, retirement and the associated loss of work roles, and loss of loved ones. The theme of loss can be pervasive with elders, particularly with frail elders. To be present to elders, we must learn to be comfortable with the expression of such losses.

Late life can be a time when grief seems overwhelming and unmanageable. It is a time of rapid change in all aspects of our lives, a time when our very roots can be shaken. It is also a time when we must reach into the core of our being, and trust in ways that we might not believe to be possible.

I believe that this struggle with loss is a school for dealing with the ultimate loss: one's own mortality. The proximity to death often increases the elders' desire to think about and discuss death. This is particularly difficult to do in a culture that defies and denies death at every turn. Again, Erik Erikson speaks eloquently to this: "The task of the elder is not simply to reaffirm life, to reinforce psychosocial strengths by maintaining meaningful involvement with people and activities. The task of the elder also includes coming to accept the inevitability of death's enforced leave taking."[9]

How can we assimilate the losses that are inherent at this stage of our life cycle? This assimilation has much to do with our value hierarchy. Arthur Becker writes that

> the role transitions called for in aging—retirement, developing a post-retirement life style, moving, and facing illness and death of oneself or spouse—are all closely related to the value hierarchy the person has developed. Gould has rightly observed that "we must do work that

confirms our talents and expresses a psychodynamic theme close to the core of us." If that central theme or value is the display of power or authority, or material gain and prosperity, then profound value shifts must be undertaken when work is laid aside. If, on the other hand, service to others, or the development of personal characteristics such as integrity, honesty, and love are the core, value shifts are not so profound.[10]

Another issue for the elder is letting go and relinquishing. We are called, in late life, to let go of past pains, hurts, and resentments. We are sometimes forced to relinquish possessions. We may be faced with letting go of a concept of ourselves that seems to be etched in stone. But this letting go can also imply movement toward God. If I could add to the Bible I would add to Ecclesiastes, "A time to acquire and a time to let go."

Meaning in Suffering

A fourth issue that is closely tied to those that we have already examined involves finding or making meaning in suffering. I believe we are called to live into our suffering and our dark moments. Many of us find that our more profound and life-changing experiences of God have been in the abyss, in the moments of suffering. In those moments when we are forced to rely on the essential love and care of our God, and when events conspire to make us forsake our ridiculous notions of control, we recognize our own powerlessness and turn to God.

Meister Eckhart tells us, "The fruit of letting go is birth," and even though I know this in my heart, I resist it bitterly. Let go; come to the edge; empty yourself so that I can fill you; my power is made perfect in weakness—we must live into an uncontrollable, unknown future if redemption is to take place. We are called, over and over, by a loving God, to suffer and to let go. This is to dance within the storm, to let our weakness bless us and, perhaps, even bless those around us.

Like everyone, elders have questions about the meaning of suffering. In the midst of chronic disease, sometimes unremitting pain, and an unknown future, how can we find or make meaning? Suffering is, and always will be, a mystery that is more complicated when you believe in the presence of a loving, merciful God.

My answer to this question is incomplete, but I have learned all of what I know about this from my elderly friends. All I can hope to do is find comfort in God's stead-fast presence in my life over time and in the rituals that sustain me. All I can do is look for reminders of resurrec-tion in my life, in the past, and in the lives of others. All I can do is remind myself that I walk every day on the edge of the abyss, but God walks with me and has even gone before me. There is a line from Madeleine L'Engle's book *The Irrational Season* that I use very often, almost as a mantra: "But I am walking with a lamb, and all the tears that ever were are gently dried on his soft fur." The God that was made known in Jesus Christ does not leave us during the suffering and the winter of our hearts. The gospel teaches us much about suffering creatively. It teach-es us that all of life is "on loan."

We also tend to confuse pain with pathology in this culture. Rather than treating suffering as a pathology that can be treated and cured, suffering must be seen as a mystery to be acknowledged and coped with. Suffering is rooted in the soul, in our ability to love, and in the very essence of our humanness. The questions of suffering must be asked from the perspectives of faith and community if they are to build character. Instead of asking "why am I suffering?" the question must be, "how will I suffer?" Will I draw closer to my brothers and sisters? Will I draw closer to my God? Who will be with me on this journey?

Brewi and Brennan write, "One finds one's story, one's calling, one's true vocation in the midst of one's broken body, one's broken dreams, one's shattered self."[11] The wilderness times of our lives are best faced in community. In community, we are enabled to "walk and not faint," and even when we do faint, we know that there are loving hands there to pick us up and brush us off. We experience being held up by community simply by the power of presence.

And, of course, encountering our limitations is always a reminder of the ultimate limitation: death. As a society, we spend an inordinate amount of time and energy denying this central reality of life. And it is such an expensive denial; it demeans us; we lose so much of what it means to be alive by denying that one day we will be dead. Death remains taboo in polite conversation, and we continue to try to divorce ourselves from it; separating ourselves from death rather than facing and embracing our mortality.

If we look intentionally at our own mortality and what it has to teach us, we find important lessons. After experiencing a life-threatening heart attack, Abraham Maslow wrote: "Death, and its ever present possibility, makes love, passionate love, more possible." The reality of death must be faced if we are to learn how to live. Scott Peck writes in *The Road Less Traveled*: "If we can live with the knowledge that death is our constant companion, traveling on our left shoulder, then death can become in the words of Don Juan 'our ally'; still fearsome, but continually a source of wise counsel."[12] I believe that when I die, I will be asked the questions that John Steinbeck poses to us, "Have I lived enough? Have I loved enough?"

Ways to Serve

Another issue for the elder is finding ways to be of service; how to give something to others, regardless of physical or mental condition. There are tremendous gifts to be offered even among the most frail. The issue of vocation in late life must be addressed by us in the spiritual context of our baptismal vows, vows that have no time limit!

Erikson's notion of "grand generativity," is a giving back to the community, a selfless contribution to the common good. Elders do this through their roles as aging parents, grandparents, mentors, and old friends. Erikson characterizes this as "concern for life itself in the face of death itself." This echoes the Whiteheads' concept of the elder as steward: "The aging steward exercises non-possessive care." They go on to say that the steward is "responsible for handing on this faith."[13]

2　Lessons Learned and Spirituality Practiced

This work results in some lessons of late life that are among the most important of the life cycle. In learning relative poverty, sometimes through the harsh stripping away of possessions and health, we can learn what is truly important; our connections with God and with our brothers and sisters.

—We can learn that our worth is not dependent on the external, but rather on the relationships we nurture and sustain.

—We learn that God's covenant promise to us is a timeless, limitless promise, and our awareness of this can deepen and ripen our time. We learn that we are on a lifelong journey toward the God who calls us by name and wants to gather us close to God's self.

—In learning reconciliation and forgiveness, we learn to live with what we cannot change, to accept the shortcomings of ourselves and others, and we can learn a sense of joy in simply experiencing the utter gift of life.

—We can learn a sense of gratefulness, which is a mark of health, both psychologically and spiritually. The elders I have known who have taught me the most have been habitually grateful.

—In recognizing our weakness, we can learn to give up our misleading notions of independence. We must learn a new paradigm of interdependence. We can learn that we are all strong and weak, all whole and broken, and that the only way we can thrive on this journey is to recognize this paradox and learn to both give and take assistance freely. We must learn to walk together as a pilgrim people.

—We can learn to accept our own powerlessness, while reminding ourselves of God's promises. Our God does not promise us an easy life or an easy old age, free from hardship. But what is promised is God's presence in the midst of the pain and the darkness. We are promised that God will never leave us alone; the gospel continually reaffirms this. God promises to be there in the darkness with us with a love that is real, tangible, and life-giving. We are reminded by Anthony De Mello that, "The final power is to be at home with powerlessness." And, if we are very wise, we can learn courage, tenacity, and hope.

—We can learn what Kathleen Fischer calls "winter grace." She writes, "Winter grace is courage grown larger in the face of diminishment."[14]

The paradoxical nature of late life is readily apparent. Growth and decline, weakness and strength, departing from and arriving, inward and outward journey; all these make up the incredible bittersweet quality of late life. This paradox is summed up in this quote from Ronald Blythe in *The View in Winter*: "Old age is full of death and full of life. It is a tolerable achievement and it is a disaster. It transcends desire and it taunts it. It is long enough and it is far from being long enough."[15]

What we are faced with is a third-age spirituality that beckons us to give up the rewards of earlier stages of life for the possibility of rewards at the final stage. This is a spirituality that asks us to take seriously, "a time to acquire and a time to let go." As the body of Christ, we must seriously and intentionally explore what this third-age spirituality calls us to do and become. A spirituality of late life must

—help people to deal with issues they face, day-in and day-out. It must help them struggle with their limitations and deal with unfinished business and broken dreams. It must help them look for meaning as they confront the experience of their limitations. Our sense of being the beloved children of God can create hopefulness even in the rapid change that we might face in our late lives.

—give older people the space and the opportunity to tell their stories and to integrate their personal stories with the larger story of community and gospel.

—help older people develop the capacity to intergenerate or mentor, through using their gifts and influence to serve others. We are called in late life to discern our gifts and offer them for the good of others. The church must be the place where elders can explore their giftedness; it is also critical that we develop rituals to mark the offerings of these gifts. We must explore potential ministries of prayer, inter-generation, hospitality, teaching, peacemaking, and social activism within the context of the church. A dear elder friend of mine, Dr. Frank Edwin, has stated, "My conception of the life cycle is this: youth is for fun and learning, adulthood is for family and work, but late life is for commitment and service to others."

—assist elders in dealing with the challenge of integrity, by giving them avenues through story sharing to deal with their unfinished business. Who we are as children of God has as much to do with our errors, wrong turns, and missed opportunities as it does with our successes and celebrations.

—assist elders in actively and intentionally developing their spiritual legacies as a contribution to their families and communities.

—help elders to understand their worth in simply "being" as

opposed to "doing." Their worth is not dependent on the possessions and status they have accumulated, their American Express Gold Card, or the lengths of their résumés, but rather on who they are, and whose they are.

—help older persons to admit (and celebrate) interdependence, knowing that the gospel calls us to this kind of connectedness within the body of Christ.

—help elders to move toward reconciliation with self, others, and God. Norman Cousins reminds us, "Life is an adventure in forgiveness." The gospel reminds us that we must both forgive and open ourselves to the healing power of being forgiven.

—help elders avoid the temptations of the narcissism that is so rampant in our culture by holding them accountable to the larger community of the church. The bumper sticker, "I'm spending my children's inheritance," is frightening. The gospel calls us to the ongoing work of creation, and a lifetime of work that will contribute to the coming of Christ's kingdom.

—help elders face death and affirm everlasting life with the belief that we are part of the kingdom of God. It has to be a spirituality which reinforces that, while mortality is a reality, it is redeemable.

A friend of mine, Father Jerry Stadel of the Episcopal Diocese of Southwest Florida, coined an important term when he referred to aging as a "subversive activity." It truly is countercultural because it flies in the face of what this culture values: the body beautiful, status, power, wealth, quickness of pace. But, when you stop to consider it, the call of the Christian gospel is also strongly countercultural. The secular world tells us to be independent at all costs; the gospel says that interdependence and community are essential marks of Jesus' people. The gospel tells us that sometimes we will carry our brothers and sisters, but certainly there will be times when we must allow ourselves to be carried by them. The gospel also admonishes us to recognize, and even celebrate, our utter dependence on the Lord of grace.

The world tells us that the person who dies with the most toys wins and that status and possessions are the marks of success. Jesus tells us, "No. The beloved of my heart are those who die with an open hand and an open heart."

The world tells us to work hard to hide our suffering, our wounds, our infirmities, because, after all, others will only exploit our weaknesses. The gospel says to show the world your wounds; bless others with your brokenness. And remember that "my power is always made perfect in weakness." Barbara Brown Taylor writes, "The Christ is not the undefeated champion; He is the suffering servant, the broken one, who comes into His glory with His wounds still visible. Those hurt places are the proof that He is who He says He is, because the way you recognize the Christ—and His followers—is not by their muscles but by their scars."[16]

The world says, "Keep it together, keep everything under control." The gospel tells us to give up our ridiculous notion of control. It never works. Aging offers us a powerful opportunity to see inklings of the coming of the kingdom. It offers the church a chance to affirm that the promises of Christ have no time limit and that our work of ministry extends from our baptisms to our deaths.

The demographic revolution that we are witnessing gives the body of Christ an opportunity to address meaningful issues that are vital to our well-being as the human family; issues of the relative worth of productivity, the meaning of suffering, the meaning of death, the meaning of caregiving, and the potential for a new paradigm of interdependence in our families and communities. This is an important work of ministry, not just for those who are already the elders in our midst. It is vital also for those of us who are traveling the road to elderhood. I have long believed that midlife should be the school for late life. If I want to be a grace-filled old woman, I must begin practicing the lessons of late life now. I must begin to face the regrets and unfinished business in my life. If I want to be an old woman whose life shows fruitfulness and the presence of Christ, I must begin to grapple with changing patterns of relating and self-concept now in midlife. Elders can perform a crucial ministry in helping those of us in midlife to have models for a grace-filled late life. We need models of aging gracefully; remaining open to life, love, and the spirit of God in spite of loss and limitation.

The church has a tremendous responsibility to address the issues of meaning that this demographic revolution confronts us with. Again, Jung is instructive. He says: "The second half of life is the spiritual work, the questions of meaning. . . . A human being would certainly not grow to be seventy or eighty years old if this longevity had no meaning for the species to which he belongs."[17]

The challenge to elders is to demonstrate the impact of a faith that can stand up to the test of time, to live "irresistibly"; to make the claims of Christ credible; to make the gospel believable. The challenge is also to transcend the self. Elders must help us to "ponder anew what the Almighty can do."

Exercises for Spiritual Reflection

Spirituality is a very personal matter since it deals with a person's relationship to God and others. This is especially true for older people who cherish their privacy. You may read this book in private, and use the following questions to guide your reflection. Or you may prefer to form a group to study the book, and use the questions as a basis for discussion.[18]

Issues of Spirituality in the Third Age
From your experience, think of two older people you know, or have known. How are they alike?

How are they different?

How do you understand the distinction between Jung's program for "life's morning and life's afternoon"? (p. 1)

Can you relate this to your own experience? If so, how?

The Life Review
Søren Kierkegaard wrote, "Life is lived forward, but it is understood backward." What do you think he meant?

How can understanding your past prepare you for a more meaningful future?

Try and recall some of your worst memories. What were they?

Can you now discern God's presence in these worst memories? If so, how?

The author tells us that older people need to face "the secrets of their past" in the context of a supportive environment. Can the church provide such an environment?

Can you think of "meaningful coincidences," i.e., when you were at the right place at the right time and things were never the same?

Do you now believe that God was at work in these events? If so, how?

The Crisis of Integrity Versus Despair
On page 4 the author describes Erikson's issue of late-life spirituality, the crisis between integrity and despair. Can you think of an older person who seems to be in despair? Why is this person in despair?

On the other hand, what older person comes to mind who epitomizes integrity and wholeness in the later years?

How can the church help free older people from despair and help them discover integrity?

Stress, Loss, and Limits
If you are an older person, list five of the losses you have already experienced, then prioritize them 1–5 (1 being the most difficult).
1.
2.
3.
4.
5.

If you are not an older person, imagine what would be the five most difficult five losses you would face in older age. Prioritize them.
1 .
2.
3 .
4.
5.

Letting Go
You are an older person who has lived forty years in the same home and now must go to a retirement community. What are some of the "relinquishing issues" you would face?

How would an active person who retires and is stripped of his or her identity at work, and deprived of work colleagues, deal with this kind of letting go? How could the person find meaningful vocations and friends in this new lifestyle?

How can the church help people who are relocating to retirement communities or assisted-living housing?

Meaning in Suffering
The author claims that "Many of us find that our more profound and life-changing experiences of God have been in the abyss, in the moment of suffering."
Try and recall biblical stories that illustrate this (e.g., Psalms, Job).

From your own life experience, can you recall an experience when God has become most real in a time of suffering?

The author urges us "to let our limping bless us, . . . even bless those around us." Relate this statement to the experience of Jacob at Peniel (Genesis 32:22–32).

Can you think of experiences in your life that left wounds that later blessed your life and others?

Can you recall "broken places in your life" that became moments of new beginning?

Plato said, "Practice dying." How can awareness of our mortality become a teacher for the later years?

Ways to Serve
In what ways can older people be "aging stewards"?

The author mentions qualities that depict a spirituality of aging. Among them are reconciliation, gratitude, interdependence, and courage. Can you describe an older person who is a model of these traits?

The apostle Paul describes spirituality as "the fruit of the Spirit" (Galatians 5:22, 23). Notice his understanding of the spiritual life. Words used to describe the spiritual life include: love, joy, peace, patience, kindness, generosity, faithfulness, gentleness, and self-control. Do you see these reflected in an older person you know? If so, how?

The author claims that "midlife should be a school for late life," and elders can perform a crucial ministry in helping those of us in midlife to have models for a grace- filled life. How can the church provide such a school for late life in its ministry?

The following prayer of an older woman was attributed to a seventeenth-century nun. Do you think this represents an older person growing in grace?

Lord, you know better than I know myself that I am growing older, and will someday be old. Keep me from being too talkative and particularly from the fatal habit of thinking that I must say something on every subject and on every occasion. Release me from craving to straighten out everybody's affairs. Make me thoughtful, but not moody; helpful, but not bossy. With my vast store of wisdom, it seems a pity not to use it all, but you know Lord, that I want a few friends at the end. Keep my mind from the recital of endless details—give me wings to come to the point. I ask for grace enough to listen to the tales of others' pain, but seal my lips on my own aches and pains. They are increasing, and my love of rehearsing them is becoming sweeter as the years go by. Help me endure them with patience. I dare not ask for improved memory but for a growing humility and a lessening cocksureness when my memory seems to clash with the memory of others. Teach me the glorious lesson that occasionally it is possible that I might be mistaken. Keep me reasonably sweet. I do not ask to be a saint—some of them are so hard to live with—but a sour old woman is one of the crowning works of the devil! Give me the ability to see good things in unexpected places, and talents in unexpected people. And give me grace, O Lord, the grace to tell them so.

Notes

1. Carl Jung, *Modern Man in Search of a Soul* (New York: Harcourt, Brace, 1933), 108.

2. Kathleen Fischer, *Winter Grace* (Mahwah, N.J.: Paulist Press, 1985), 34.

3. Arthur Becker, *Ministry with Older Persons* (Minneapolis: Augsburg Publishing House, 1985), 104.

4. Jane Thibault, *A Deepening Love Affair* (Nashville: Upper Room Press, 1994), 152.

5. Frederick Buechner, *Whistling in the Dark* (New York: Harper & Row, 1988), 103–4.

6. M. Lewis and R. Butler, "Life Review Therapy: Putting Meaning to Work in Individual and Group Therapy," *International Journal of Aging and Human Development* 5 (1974): 287.

7. May Sarton, *At Seventy: A Journal* (New York: W. W. Norton & Co., 1984), 77.

8. Erik Erikson, *Childhood and Society* (New York: W. W. Norton & Co., 1963), 268.

9. Ibid.

10. Becker, *Ministry with Older Persons*, 57.

11. J. Brewi and A. Brennan, *Celebrate Midlife* (New York: Crossroad, 1988), 122.

12. M. Scott Peck, *The Road Less Traveled* (New York: Simon & Schuster, 1978), 61.

13. Evelyn and James Whitehead, *Seasons of Strength* (New York: Image Books, 1984), 53.

14. Kathleen Fischer, *Winter Grace*, rev. ed. (Nashville: Upper Room Books, 1997).

15. Ronald Blythe, *The View in Winter* (New York: Harcourt, Brace, Jovanovich, 1979), 29.

16. Barbara Brown Taylor, *Gospel Medicine* (Boston: Cowley, 1995), 2.

17. Jung, *Modern Man in Search of a Soul*, 109.

18. See Richard L. Morgan, *Remembering Your Story: A Leader's Guide* (Nashville: Upper Room Books, 1996) for a helpful approach to group sharing of stories. Sharing secrets can be done in a group, building trust and confidentiality, or with a trusted spiritual friend.

Suggested Reading

Becker, Arthur. *Ministry with Older Persons*. Minneapolis, Minn.: Augsburg Publishing House, 1986.

Blythe, R. *The View in Winter*. New York: Harcourt, Brace, Jovanovich, 1979.

Brewi, Janice, and A. Brennan. *Celebrate Mid-Life*. New York: Crossroad, 1988.

Brown, Barbara Taylor. *Gospel Medicine*. New York: Cowley Press, 1995.

Buechner, Frederick. *Whistling in the Dark*. New York: Harper & Row, 1988.

Cousins, Norman. *Anatomy of an Illness*. New York: W. W. Norton & Co., 1979.

Erikson, Erik, Joan Erikson, and H. Kivnich. *Vital Involvement in Old Age*. New York: W. W. Norton & Co., 1986.

Fischer, Kathleen. *Winter Grace: Spirituality for Later Years*. Nashville: Upper Room Books, 1997 (revised).

Jung, Carl G. *Memories, Dreams, and Reflections*. New York: Vintage Press, 1989.

L'Engle, Madeleine. *The Irrational Season*. New York: Harper & Row, 1974.

Magee, James J. *A Professional's Guide to Older Adults' Life Review*. New York: Lexington Books, 1988.

Morgan, Richard L. *Remembering Your Story*. Nashville: Upper Room Books, 1996.

Peck, Scott. *The Road Less Traveled*. New York: Simon & Schuster, 1978.

Sarton, May. *At Seventy: A Journal*. New York: W. W. Norton & Co., 1984.

Thibault, Jane. *A Deepening Love Affair*. Nashville: Upper Room Books, 1993.

Whitehead, Evelyn, and James Whitehead. *Seasons of Strength*. New York: Image Books, 1984.

For Further Study

The following books deal with spirituality as seen through the eyes of elders.

Burt, Donald. *But When You Are Old: Reflections on Coming to Age.* Collegeville, Minn.: Liturgical Press, 1992.

Cowley, Malcolm. *The View from 80.* New York: Viking Press, 1976.

Fisher, M. F. K. *Sister Age.* New York: Vantage Books, 1984.

Folliet, Joseph. *The Evening Sun: Growing Old Beautifully.* Chicago: Franciscan Herald Press, 1983.

Geissler, Eugene. *The Best Is Yet to Be: Life's Meaning in the Aging Years.* Notre Dame, Ind.: Ave Maria Press, 1988.

MacDonald, George. *Diary of an Old Soul.* Minneapolis: Augsburg Publishing House, 1975.

Millner, Nancy Bost. *Creative Aging.* Palo Alto, Calif.: Davis-Black, 1998.

Missine, Leo. *Reflections on Aging: A Spiritual Guide.* St. Louis, Mo.: Liguori Publications, 1990.

Morgan, Richard L. *No Wrinkles on the Soul: A Book of Readings for Older Adults.* Nashville: Upper Room Books, 1990.

———. *Autumn Wisdom.* Nashville: Upper Room Books, 1994.

Morrison, Mary C. *Let Evening Come: Reflections on Aging*. New York: Doubleday, 1998.

Raines, Robert. *A Time to Live: Seven Tasks of Creative Aging*. New York: Dutton, 1997.

Reilly, Maria. *Now That I Am Old. Meditations on the Meaning of Life*. Mystic, Conn.: Twenty-Third Publications, 1994.

Scott-Maxwell, Florida. *The Measure of My Days*. New York: Alfred A. Knopf, 1968.

Valentine, Mary. *Aging in the Lord*. Mahwah, N.J.: Paulist Press, 1994.

Vining, Elizabeth G. *Being Seventy: The Measure of a Year*. New York: Viking Press, 1978.

Wallis, Velma. *Two Old Women*. Seattle, Wash.: Epicenter Press, 1993.